clarifying purposes only and are the owned by the owners themselves, not affiliated with this document.

Success

How the Most Dangerous Men on the Planet Succeed and Win!

John Collins

Table of Contents

Introduction

Navy SEAL 40% Rule

US Navy SEALs strongly believe that we all have a reserve tank. Only when we are pushed to the limits can we find out what we really have in the tank. SEALs say that when you hit a road block, when you've hit your quit and when you feel done you still have another 40% left to go. With this mindset they stretch far beyond their mental and physical limitations. This takes hard work and preparation to another level and separates them from the competition.

"Everybody has a plan until they get punched in the face."

Many people think that success is tied to having a clear plan for the work they are trying to accomplish. While it is helpful to have a plan, that plan is only going to go so far, and it is only going to last so long. Rather than a plan, what you really need is a strategy. A strategy is an overriding theme to how you are going to approach the task at hand. Where a detailed step-by-step plan can easily come apart or need to change as soon as you get started, a strategy is something that you can see out all the way to the end of the job.

Do you think everything goes exactly according to plan when the US Navy SEALs engage an enemy in order to achieve a specific objective? No way. The battlefield is a scary and a difficult place, and it is always filled with surprises. So while the SEALs have a plan in place when they start, they also have a number of contingencies ready that they can enact in order to stick with their overall strategy. At the end of the day, the idea is to successfully complete the overall mission – the plan that is taken to reach that goal ultimately isn't relevant to the outcome.

"The Only Easy Day Was Yesterday".

US Navy SEALs use this saying because it perfectly describes what it is to be a SEAL. Yesterday was tough, sure, but today is going to be tougher. That's why yesterday is framed as 'easy'. Was yesterday actually easy for the SEALs. No – it wasn't. But today is going to be harder, and tomorrow is going to be even harder still. When you approach life with this mindset, you stop searching for easy and you begin to accept and embrace the difficult.

On the road to success, you can't be looking for easy days. Those who are successful in this world – no matter what they happen to be successful in – don't look for easy days. Instead, while others are taking their easy days to rest and recover, the successful are pushing on, finding a way to improve themselves one step at a time. Is it easy? Of course not. Is it rewarding? Absolutely.

As you set about the process of taking your life in the directions that you want to go, think carefully about the motto that 'the only easy day was yesterday'. If you can adopt that way of thinking, you will find that you continually make yourself better, and you continually get closer to your goals. Most people, unfortunately, approach life with the opposite view. They hope that the easy days are waiting ahead, and they want the hard work to be over. The hard work is never over.

The dictionary definition of the word success is 'the accomplishment of an aim or purpose'. Using that definition, it is easy to say that SEALs are some of the most-successful people on the planet. They are famous for accomplishing their missions time after time, even when those missions might seem impossible to a 'regular' person. SEALs are tough, disciplined, resilient, loyal, and yes, successful.

Another one of the great SEAL sayings is 'we're not going to stop until we get at least one quitter!' This is used during training as the weak are being weeded out from the strong. This process takes place every day in real life, just as it does in SEAL training. Are you going to be the weak one who quits, or are you going to stick it out to the end?

So, is it possible to learn from the Navy SEALs and apply their mindset to your own life? It certainly is. Even if you aren't going to get anywhere near a battlefield, you can still improve your day to day life by taking the way the SEALs approach their work and applying it to your own purposes. From trying to climb the corporate ladder to building a better life at home and everything in between, the principles for becoming successful don't change.

Chapter One - Why a US Navy SEAL?

As you are looking for inspiration and motivation to be the best you can be, and to succeed as frequently as possible, why would you look to the Navy SEALs? Why use them for your template of success?

The better question, instead of why, might be *why not*? The SEALs are winners in every sense of the word, and patterning your behaviors after their attributes is sure to lead to great results.

There are few tasks in the world that are quite as challenging from both a physical and mental standpoint than what is required to become a SEAL. No matter what you are going through in your professional life, it is likely to pale in comparison to the demands placed on the SEALs. They are going to be going to battle in some of the most difficult environments imaginable, so they are put to the test right from the moment they enter the program.

Understanding BUD/S

You probably are vaguely familiar with some of the things that SEALs are required to do in order to earn their spot. Specifically, Hell Week is a well-known (and feared) part of the process. However, it is important to understand that Hell Week is only a small part of the overall training known as BUD/S, or Basic Underwater Demolition/SEAL. In total, this is a six-month training course that is held in Southern California, and it is meant to push each and every participant to the very limit of what they are capable of achieving.

At the heart of this process is the need to weed out the weak from the field of potential SEALs (more on this concept later). Everything that the BUD/S training asks of each individual will help to determine if they are actually up to the task of being a SEAL. The physical challenge is incredibly steep, and the mental challenge may be even steeper. Only those who can attack the BUD/S process with a strong body and a sound and committed mind will be able to make it out on the other side after a brutal six months.

Once the indoctrination and pre-training process is complete, which takes five weeks, the first phase of BUD/S begins. This is considered the most-difficult part of the process, and it lasts for eight weeks, one of which is the infamous Hell Week. Some of the physical tasks that are asked of potential SEALs during this time include four mile timed run in boots, running in the sand, swimming up to two miles in the ocean, and more. Once Hell Week is under way, training is required for 5 ½ days straight, with only four hours of sleep total! Most people feel fatigued if they only get four hours of sleep in a single night – let alone getting that amount of sleep over the period of a week while undergoing constant physical training.

How hard is it to survive the first phase of BUD/S? It is common for two-thirds of a class to drop out before the eight weeks are completed. For those who do survive and see it through to the finish, there will be mixed emotions – a sense of pride for having survived week one is deserved, but there is also a sense of dread that another 17 weeks of BUD/S lies ahead over the course of phases two and three. Some of the skills and challenges that are dealt with in those phases include SCUBA diving, combat swimming, weapons training, rappelling, and much more.

What It Takes to Survive

It doesn't take much imagination to understand just how incredibly demanding the BUD/S training program is for potential SEALs. Even one day of this kind of training would break the 'average Joe', so it takes something special to keep coming back for more day after day for six months. Those who graduate the program will have earned the respect of their peers for the impressive effort required to reach that elusive finish line.

Understanding what it takes to reach the end of BUD/S training will provide you a great look inside the mind of a SEAL, and you will be able to take that kind of thinking into your own life as you face your own challenges. While most of the focus is on what the SEALs have to do physically to get through BUD/S, it is really the mental half of the equation that determines success or failure. The human body is capable of far more than the mind realizes in most cases, so it is a matter of mind over matter for most SEAL candidates. Some of the most-physically fit people in the world have failed in BUD/S training, simply because they didn't have the focus, determination, and drive to see it through to the end.

This is really where the average person can learn from a SEAL. Most likely, you are never going to be put through any kind of rigorous physical training during your life. Even if you are someone that keeps yourself in good physical condition, you probably aren't going to have to put that conditioning to the test in the toughest conditions imaginable. So, when it comes to watching how the SEALs perform and how they succeed, it is the mental side of the picture that can be incredibly valuable. SEALs live up to the word 'success' by every possible definition, so moving yourself closer to their standard will help you drive closer toward success in your own life.

Why the Weak Are Weeded Out from the Strong

It could be said that the BUD/S training program that the SEALs are forced to endure doesn't build character - rather, it reveals it. That is the underlying idea behind all of this crazy training that these individuals are subjected to during the six-month course. Do the leaders of the SEAL program set up these challenges simply because they want to see the candidates suffer? Of course not. There is a method to the madness. The only way to determine if someone is worthy of the title of SEAL is to put them to the test. In the process of completing these challenges, the weak will be pulled from the field, and only the strong will survive to the end.

There is one critical reason why the weak need to be weeded out from the strong during training, and that is to make sure that the weak never wind up undermining a critical mission out in the battlefield. If the training program was anything less than brutal, there may be individuals who slip through the process without really possessing what it takes to be a SEAL. That would be an outcome which could literally have fatal consequences. SEALs are in life and death situations regularly in the field, so each member of the team has to be as strong as possible in order to keep everyone safe. A chain is only as strong as the weakest link - and there is no room for even a single weak link within the ranks of the SEALs.

Pulling the weak out of the strong through a process like the BUD/s training program is not only good for the SEALs as a whole, but it is also good for those who don't complete the training. Having an individual earn the title of SEAL who is really not up to the task would be a disaster for that individual, as they would then be put in positions that could quickly compromise their safety. As painful as it might be at the time, identifying someone as falling short of the SEAL title is actually in that person's best interest, as well as being in the best interest of the team.

The Definition of Mental Toughness

SEAL's are some of the most mentally strong individuals in the world. They possess the ability to place 'mind over matter' and achieve success no matter what extreme conditions or difficulties they may face. This is, again, at the heart of BUD/S. Only those who have the appropriate level of mental toughness, along with the requisite physical abilities, will be the ones who last.

Mental Toughness can be broken down into 4 areas. These areas are goal setting, visualization, positive self-talk, and arousal control.

Goal Setting – SEALs break down their goals into micro goals, short-term goals, mid-term goals, and long-term goals. Instead of thinking of completing the six month training course as one goal, those who graduated BUD/S broke down the six months into weekly goals, daily goals, hourly goals, and even goals by the minute. Setting extremely short-term and specific goals allows the mind to focus on one thing at a time. More focus means better results.

Visualization – This has been used by Olympic athletes and world class musicians for quite some time. As a matter of fact, some psychologists think that mental practice is just as important as actual practice itself. SEALs use visualization to calm themselves in dangerous situations and to connect with the finish line before it happens. This constant visualization serves to prepare the mind for what is to come. When the mind perseveres, the body usually follows.

Positive Self-Talk - Those who graduate from BUD/S block out all doubt and only use the concept of positive self-talk to constantly push themselves forward. Many SEALS remind themselves constantly that many men before them have completed the course and so can they. They remind themselves to go on and never quit, no matter what. Because every minute of BUD/S training is a test of mental fortitude, SEALS have to constantly use self-talk, sometimes every few minutes to keep it together. Having positive self-talk often serves as a constant reminder to bite down and persevere.

Control of Arousal - Controlling your mental state is extremely important to being mentally resilient. SEALS are able to control their physiological and psychological response when aroused by outside stimuli (such as danger). When our bodies feel overwhelmed or in danger, it releases chemicals known as cortisol and endorphin. It is these chemicals that cause our palms to sweat, our minds to race, our hearts to pound, and our bodily functions to malfunction. This is the body's natural response to stress, developed over millions of years of human evolution. But SEALS learn to control this natural response to arousal so that they are poised even under the most stressful of circumstances.

One method that is taught to SEALS to control arousal is the 4×4 breathing technique. You begin by inhaling deeply for 4 seconds and follow with four seconds of steady exhaling. This must be done for a minimum of 1 minute to be effective in controlling arousal.

"It was never about physical strength, Wit Reminded himself. It was 90 percent mental, 10 percent physical. That's what the SEAL instructors were looking for: soldiers who could disregard the pleadings of the body. Pain was nothing. Sleep was nothing. What was chaffed skin, wrecked muscles and bleeding sores? The body chooses to be sore. The body chooses to be exhausted. But the SEAL mind rejects it. The SEAL mind commands the body, not the other way around." – Unknown

Block Negative Self-Talk

If mental toughness is the ability to fight through difficult circumstances and come out on the other site, negative self-talk is the exact opposite of that. Instead of constantly telling yourself that 'you can do it' even in the face of adversity, you will easily give up when you have a negative stream of thoughts running through your mind. Those who are plagued with negative thoughts are easily defeated, and they rarely accomplish any goals that they have set for themselves. Simply put, "Doubt kills the warrior."

This is the polar opposite of the Navy SEAL approach to life. Where SEALs will always work hard to find a way to win in the end, negative thinkers grab on to the first opportunity to quit. Of course, if a SEAL was prone to this kind of thinking, he never would have become a SEAL to begin with.

In the world of SEAL training, negative self-talk could take a number of forms. On a long run, a candidate could tell themselves that they have a pain in their knee and they should stop. During a swim, they could decide that they are cold and they need to get out of the water. No matter what it is, whatever is playing in your mind can always override what your body is trying to accomplish. If you have the self-doubt soundtrack on repeat in the back of your mind, you are never going to reach your goals.

In the 'real' world, negative self-talk can be just as damaging as it would be during SEAL training. For the new business owner, one bad month of sales could set off a habit of negative self-talk that leads to eventually giving up on the dream. For a student, a single bad grade or bad score on a test could undermine confidence and lead that student to come up short of graduation. In any field and with any goal, negative self-talk can be an incredibly destructive force.

Learn to Run - from the SEALs?

If there is one group of people who you would never expect to run away, it would be the US NAVY SEALs. They are known to be some of the baddest men on the planet, and it would seem that they are the types that would rather die trying than give in or give up. Most people would never expect to seal them raise the white flag or hightail it out of battle.

However, that is exactly what is required in some circumstances. Being a SEAL is all about making strategic choices to achieve the objective. Avoiding bad situations is as important as finding good situations when it comes to being successful. Being dead doesn't get them closer to reaching the objective. When SEALs find themselves in an unwinnable position, rather than make the gallant effort at a last stand they will retreat into a safe position where they can reassess the situation and develop a better plan.

It is important to recognize that 'running away' does not mean giving up. You can run away from a specific situation without giving up on your overall objective. In the SEAL world, it means that they will "Live to fight another day." It simply means regrouping and reassembling to come up with a new strategy that is going to make them successful in the future. In the business world, that might mean backing away from one side of your business that is challenging you so you can focus on another, more successful part of it. You aren't giving up on your dream as a whole - you are simply realigning things along the way to ensure a successful outcome. The path to success is never a clear and straight one, and there is a good chance that you are going to have to 'run away' while on your journey.

Chapter Two - The Power of Purpose

What do you do with your days? Do you have a purpose in what you do, or are you just spending time without any real direction? If you want to be successful, everything you do will have a specific and important purpose attached to it.

As you would guess, the SEALs don't waste time. Everything they do has meaning, purpose, and importance. Whether it is the BUD/S training process which is designed to weed out the weak and prepare the rest for battle, or an actual mission where they are trying to accomplish an objective, the SEALs mean business. Unfortunately, if you are like most people, your regular day to day life does not have the same purpose and passion that is demonstrated by the SEALs.

To get yourself pointed in the right direction, and to put some purpose in your life, ask yourself the following question -

What would you need to accomplish in order to consider yourself a success?

That is a simple question, yet it is very complicated at the same time. As we are all individuals with unique goals and perspectives on life, your answer to that question will be specific to you personally. In fact, you could ask that question to ten different people and get ten very different answers. There is, of course, no right or wrong with that question. As long as you have a clear definition of what you would feel is success in your life, you can work hard toward that end.

For some people, money will be what they look to in order to define success. Making a specific amount of money within a year, or having a certain amount of money stored in the bank, will make them feel successful. For others, achieving a certain professional title or other accomplishment will be what it takes. Also, for a large number of people, success will be defined by creating a family and spending time with that family on a regular basis. No matter what it is that you feel will make you successful, don't be afraid of it, and don't feel the need to be something you're not. It doesn't matter if your definition of success is different than that of others - as long as it motivates you and gives you purpose each day when you get out of bed.

Why is as Important as What

Now that you know what it is that motivates you, and what you would consider a success, you need to think about why those things matter to you. This can be a difficult point to get your head around at first, but it will become extremely important as you work toward your goals. You not only need to have the 'what' in place as your ultimate goal, but you need to have the 'why' component in place as well. The 'what' is your ultimate goal and it will define your success or failure, but the 'why' half of the puzzle is going to be your motivation. A goal without motivation is never going to be realized, but a goal with clear and strong motivation will soon be accomplished.

It is easy to be charged up and excited when you first set a goal for yourself. For example, if you enroll in classes in order to eventually receive a Master's degree in your field, you will likely start out in those classes with plenty of excitement for what is to come. Even if you aren't looking forward to doing the work, the reward at the end of the process will make it worth the sacrifice. This initial excitement is great to get you started - however, it is unlikely to last for long.

Inevitably, the mundane routine of everyday life will start to take its toll and you will lose track of your motivation for reaching the goal you had initially set out to achieve. Even though you still want to reach that goal, it will be harder and harder to drive yourself forward each day. Some days you will feel tired and you won't want to do much work. Other days you may feel under the weather and would rather stay in bed. There will always be issues that come up, because real life is challenging and demanding. Only the strong will make it through to be successful in pursuit of their goals.

This is why it is so important to have a clear and unwavering motivation in your life. The 'why' part of the equation is the emotional component, and it has the power to rise above everything else in order to push you toward getting the job done. As an example, imagine that you have decided that making a lot of money is your main goal. Maybe you have set a mark of earning more than $100,000 in a year. That's a great goal, and it will cause you to work hard at first. However, it is just a number, and it will lose its significance to you over time. So how do you stay motivated? By thinking about what that money would mean for your everyday life. Asking yourself 'why' you want to make $100,000 in a year is as important as setting that goal in the first place.

You might decide that you want to make that much money because it will allow you to save for the future, or to buy a nice house for your family, or to travel the world to see beautiful cities and places. It doesn't matter what your 'why' happens to be, as long as it is specific and as long as it is truly important to you. For most people, the 'why' is going to be related to family, but it certainly doesn't have to be. Whatever makes you feel excited, emotional, and motivated is perfect for this purpose.

With your goals and your motivations both clearly laid out - the 'what' and the 'why' in this discussion - there will be very little that can stand in your way. A goal without motivation is unlikely to be realized, and motivation without a goal will lead to wasted energy going in a million different directions all at once. However, when both the goal and the motivation come together in a powerful package, great things can be achieved.

SEAL Motto - "Fire in the Gut"

The SEALs tend to use a lot of sayings and mottos, as they can be helpful to keep everyone on the same page and make sure everyone is working toward the same goal. One of those mottos is "fire in the gut". What does that mean? Basically, it means that you have a burning desire from within to be the best that you can possibly be. It is this 'fire' that will keep you going when times get tough. When other people would simply give up, those with a burning desire for success will push through and find a way to achieve their goals.

Do you have the necessary 'fire in the gut' to succeed in your pursuits? In many ways, this motto relates to the discussion In the previous section. By putting together a solid combination of goals and motivations, you should be able to stoke your fire and keep it burning for years to come. It is easy to spot the people in life who have a strong desire from within to see their goals out to completion - they are the ones who are living in big houses, driving nice cars, taking long vacations, and generally finding success around every corner. While it is easy to chock up other people's success to good old fashioned luck, it is more often correlated with the burning desire to be great.

Chapter Three - Be Someone Special Everyday

It is easy in life to simply 'fit in'. You can just go along with the normal path that everyone else is taking, punching the clock and earning enough money to get by. There is nothing wrong with that path - unless you have the desire to accomplish extraordinary things. If you want to stand out from the pack and reach levels that many people only dream of achieving, you are going to have to be special each and every day.

What does it mean to be 'special'? In this context, being special means being that person that everyone around you looks to for help, for support, for answers, and more. It is the leader in any situation that has the most to lose, but also the most to gain. If you are willing to put yourself out there as the leader of the pack, you could wind up reaping tremendous rewards. There is always risk when you put yourself in a position of leadership, but risk is required when valuable rewards are desired.

SEALs are Special

Without a doubt, SEALs are special individuals who have chosen a harder path in order to achieve great things in their lives. It would have been much easier to go in another direction - almost any other direction - rather than becoming a SEAL. However, what makes these people special is the fact that they don't pick the easy path. They take the harder route on purpose, knowing they will be better for it when they come out on the other side.

The mindset that the SEALs take up as part of their training and education is called 'to be unbeatable'. That motto and mindset is exactly as it sounds - the SEALs make it their goal through preparation and hard work to become unbeatable individuals and teams. Whether working on their own or as part of the group, SEALs aspire to be unbeatable in the face of any challenge. This line of thinking has a lot to do with their impressive track record of success. The SEALs rarely lose, and that is in large part because they go into every situation thinking that they are going to win. A positive mindset, in conjunction with the right training and planning, leads to positive outcomes that are rarely in doubt.

Be Reflective

A large part of becoming a person that stands out as special is a willingness to reflect on your mistakes and learn from them. In some circles, there is a misleading belief that the SEALs are somehow perfect. That simply isn't true. The SEALs, as impressive as they are, remain human just like everyone else. They make mistakes, and they have to learn from those mistakes in order to improve. Perfection simply isn't possible in the real world - but being reflective and getting better as a result of your mistakes will drive you ever closer to that unreachable target.

The difference between US NAVY SEALs and the 'average Joe' is not that the SEALs don't make mistakes - it is that SEALs are willing to take a hard look in the mirror in order to get better. It is never easy to look at one's own mistakes, and most people will turn in the other direction when confronted with their own failings. Commonly, people will simply excuse away their mistakes by blaming them on someone or something else. That is not how it works with the SEALs.

Accountability is crucial, and each mistake is examined and learned from before moving on.

If you are going to be truly successful in your life, developing the ability to reflect on your own mistakes should become one of your top priorities. We all do some things right and some things wrong as you go about day to day life. The question is, are you going to get better by learning from what you have done wrong, or are you going to turn away when faced with those failings?

Be accountable for your actions and admit when you are wrong. SEALs take full responsibility for themselves and their teams. They don't whine and they do not blame others. They win or fail all under their own merit.

Become Obsessively Organized

Organization is one of the keys to success that most people take for granted as they go about day to day life. Staying organized is a great way to boost productivity, clear your mind, and allow yourself to focus on the task at hand. Those who are successful are typically organized in both their professional and personal lives. It is extremely difficult to be great at what you do while also remaining in a constant state of clutter.

When it comes to organization, even the little things count. Don't think you need to worry about folding your clothes and putting them away? That might not seem like something that could affect your success or failure in life, but it is one small piece of a big puzzle. If your wardrobe falls into a state of disarray, the rest of your life may be soon to follow. If you cannot get the little things right, then how will you get the big things right? Take the small tasks seriously in terms of staying organized and watch how the large tasks become easier and easier.

If you think that a Navy SEAL would be living in a state of constant disruption and confusion, you are sadly mistaken. Everything that is done by these professionals is carefully monitored and meticulously cared for on an ongoing basis. A SEAL isn't going to have to look far to find his uniform, or anything else for that matter. Everything has a place, and everything is in its place. It is attention to detail that allows one to rise to the rank of Navy SEAL in the first place, and those habits certainly don't stop once that rank has been achieved.

Assume You Don't Know Enough

No one knows everything. That is a literal statement – there is no one in the world that knows everything about anything. Sure, there are various people who are experts in particular fields, but even they have their strengths and weaknesses when it comes to knowledge. If you think you know everything about any one subject, you are certain to be proven wrong at some point in the not-too-distant future.

There is something of a misconception among the public that a SEAL has finished his training when the BUD/S process is complete. Nothing could be further from the truth. In fact, the learning has just begun at that point. A Navy SEAL will be learning and growing from their first day in BUD/S training until they day they retire. Life is all about learning from your experiences as you go, and that certainly applies to a task as difficult and intimidating as being a Navy SEAL.

Those who are ultimately successful in life are the ones who are willing to set ego aside and acknowledge the fact that there is still more to learn. There is nothing wrong with having confidence in your knowledge and your ability, but that confidence needs to come along with a healthy dose of humility as well. The combination of confidence and humility is a powerful force, because it can lead to a point where you are willing to learn new skills but also confident enough to put them into use. Some of the most successful people in the world – whether they be Navy SEALs or professionals in other lines of work – have learned how to beautifully walk the line between confidence and humility. If you can do the same, great accomplishments should be laying ahead.

Keep learning. The devil is in the details. You never know when one little-known fact or detail might make all the difference in the world. There is no end to the education of a US Navy SEAL. Learning is eternal, whether it be in training or simply learning from your mistakes. Having the right mindset around continual learning is paramount for everyone.

Chapter Four - Begin with the End in Mind

Rushing into action is no way to get started on a path to success. In their haste to simply get started, many people put the proverbial 'cart in front of the horse'. The SEALs would never make this kind of mistake, and neither should you. Everything that the SEALs do in the field, or even in training, is carefully calculated and planned. While those plans might have to change once an enemy is engaged, it is still important to have a plan for success before taking any action at all.

No matter what it is that you feel will qualify as a success in your life, you need to see your path to that outcome before you start to take action. For instance, if you wish to be a business owner who can set your own hours and make your own money, you will need to have a specific plan in place to make that happen. Simply renting out a showroom and opening up for business isn't going to do any good if you don't know what you will sell or how you will get customers. Only when you have the patience and forethought to plan out your path to success will you be able to walk it in the real world.

Learning the Tool of Visualization

Visualization is a powerful tool that is used by successful people in all walks of life. Professional athletes are well-known for their ability to 'see' the action before it actually happens, meaning they are able to react quickly and appropriately. Also, you can be sure that the SEALs use visualization techniques to put themselves in the heat of battle mentally before they are ever physically in the field. The mind is a powerful tool, and it has an incredible ability to visualize even the smallest details within a given scenario.

So how can visualization help you succeed in life? By helping you be prepared. Preparation is one of the biggest keys to success, but failing to visualize situations before they arise can leave you feeling unprepared and even downright out of control. To learn visualization that you can apply in the real world, start by trying to visualize short scenarios that you may encounter within the next day. For instance, if you are expecting to have a meeting with your boss (or maybe one of your employees), visualize that meeting and picture how it might go before it actually happens. By playing through a few scenarios in your mind, you may be able to settle on the right things to say in order to work through whatever issues could arise.

Visualization is something that should be done quietly, by yourself, in a place where you can relax and focus. If you have a few minutes to yourself in the morning before you need to get your day start, this would be a perfect time to visualize the days ahead. It is more difficult to visualize properly at night when you have the stress of the day on your mind, so try to carve out early morning time if possible for this task.

See The Victory Before it Unfolds

It isn't enough to simply visualize the days that are to come – specifically, you want to visualize success. It is easy to get into a cycle of negative thinking where you picture everything going wrong. That isn't going to help you get any closer to success, and it could easily hold you back. Instead, see victories lining up one after the next. Picture everything going your way, and see what kind of great rewards you could enjoy as a result.

Just as it is important to think about being successful, it is just as important to not think about being a failure. You don't have to run away from the idea of failure, but you certainly shouldn't expect it. Everyone runs into bumps along the way in life, but that doesn't mean you are a failure or that you are going to continue to fail in the months and years to come. Each new day is a chance to be successful and reach for your goals.

Planning Your Day is Never a Waste of Time

To be successful, or even just to be productive, you don't have to be moving at all times. People tend to think of the Navy SEALs as being in a state of perpetual motion, but that simply isn't true. While they are certainly in amazing physical condition and are capable of incredibly challenging tasks, they also take time to stop, sit down, and make a plan. If you feel like you need to start your day with some time spent sitting in your favorite chair while strategizing the hours to come, you aren't wasting time at all. In fact, this is one of the best possible ways you could be spending your time, as you will then be more productive for the rest of the day as a result.

Successful people have great habits, and they are committed to those habits day after day, week after week. One of the top habits that you can use to follow a path toward success is taking time out every morning to plan your day. Even if it is only five minutes while drinking a cup of coffee, this quick break in the action may lead you to new heights. Don't feel guilty while sitting still because you are thinking about all of the things you should be doing. No one can move 24 hours a day, and spending time in thought is one of the habits that successful people – including the SEALs – use most often.

Chapter Five – SEAL Leadership for Life

Leadership is one of the most important single elements of success. Where most people think that only someone who is 'in charge' – such as the boss in a work setting – needs to be a leader. That is an incredibly misguided concept. In reality, everyone is a leader, as you can lead other people through your words and actions even if you are not in a position of power at the moment. In fact, some of the most effective leaders are those who were not given their power and influence, but rather they earned it over time by leading others to act and perform in a positive fashion.

The SEALs are a great example of this notion. While there are clearly defined roles within the SEALs, and there is a hierarchy in place, each and every one of the SEALs considers himself a leader. You don't rise to the rank of SEAL if you are unable to lead others – that simply is not a possibility. When the SEALs are out in the field, they each lead by their own example, while also following orders from their superiors. One of the best ways that the SEALs are able to lead their fellow team members is by putting their own safety behind that of the others on the team. If each person on the team is more concerned about his teammate than he is about his own security, the team as a whole will be a powerful and impressive unit.

Leaders Fail

Sound leadership is a staple of what the US Navy SEALs stand for. Great leaders have an open mind and can follow as well as lead. Their commitment to the team must come before their ego. SEALs learn that great leaders must have a competitive spirit but also be gracious when losing. SEALs are taught that the leaders are ultimately responsible for success and failure of the team. Even if the leader is not directly responsible for the outcome, it was there method of instruction and direction that led to the result. They call this extreme ownership.

A quality leader is willing to set up and admit their mistakes. Coming up short is nothing to be ashamed of, as long as the failures are acknowledged and learned from for the next situation. It isn't always easy to have the humility necessary to admit when something has gone wrong, but it is absolutely necessary to build a reputation as a great leader. No one is going to follow you if you claim to be perfect – but you can build tremendous amounts of trust and respect if you are willing to be upfront with your failings.

Communication is Key

Clear communication might be the single most important part of leading successfully. There can be no confusion between yourself and the others working around you if you are going to lead them in the right direction. SEALs are always on the same page as the rest of their team, and that cohesion is thanks to tremendous communication skills which have been developed over countless hours of training. A breakdown in communication among the SEALs could literally mean the difference between life and death, so no chances are taken whatsoever.

The stakes are likely someone less significant in your case, but it is still important that you communicate clearly. If you are serious about clearing a path for yourself to a successful future, one of the best things you can do is work on your communication skills. Be open with people, ask for feedback, and don't get defensive if you receive some criticism along the way.

One Size Does Not Fit All

Among the many lessons that you will learn as you gain experience as a leader is that you cannot treat everyone in the same manner. You should treat everyone fairly, of course, but you cannot go into each conversation with the same tone. Many people think that the SEALs are yelled at all day, every day, but there is more subtlety to it than that. In some cases, it is appropriate to be hard and stern with your tone, but other situations call for caution, care, and respect. A talented leader will have a good sense for the moment, knowing when to demand more and when to gently ask for it.

It is tempting to become a task master when acting as a leader. With people who are willing to respond to you, the temptation may be there to continue to demand more and more without offering much in return. That is a strategy that is unlikely to succeed for long in the real world. You have to respect the people you are working with, and you have to understand that they need a reason to stay motivated. Without motivation, nothing gets done and everyone fails in the end.

The ability to adapt is something that the SEALs have in spades, yet many people in everyday life like to stick in their lanes and are afraid to stray too far outside of the lines. Don't be the person who never adapts or adjusts to the times – as you are sure to be left behind. Whether it is your leadership style or just about anything else you do, adaptation is one of the keys to the Promised Land.

Follow First, Then Lead

The best way to learn how to lead is to first learn how to follow. When you follow the lead of someone who is already comfortable in that role, you will see what they offer and how it affects you as a person. That doesn't mean you need to directly copy their management style when you are in that role – you will always need to be yourself, while taking lessons in bits and pieces from others. With plenty of experience serving as a follower under your belt, you will soon feel like you can take the reins and lead with the best of the best. Navy SEALs certainly don't start out trying to take charge of the whole team, and neither should you. SEALs learn from those who came before, and they add on to what has already been accomplished one piece at a time.

Chapter Six – Never Do It Alone

No one succeeds alone. Even the most successful, most cutthroat business people rely on others to help get them where they want to go. It takes teamwork to rise to the top in any profession, and no group highlights that concept better than the SEALs. As impressive as they are individually, what makes the SEALs such an intimidating force is the way they are able to work together as a cohesive unit. As individuals, they wouldn't be able to accomplish much out in the field against an organized and powerful enemy. However, as a unit, the SEALs can conquer the world, and they are respected as one of the most capable forces in the world as a result.

Loyalty is a characteristic that is sadly lacking in today's world. There are too many people who are in it only for themselves, not understanding that the attitude of self-reliance is one that will actually get them in trouble. After all, if the SEALs are willing to work together with their teammates in order to accomplish goals, shouldn't you be willing to do the same? The world is too challenging to face alone, but it can be met with confidence when you are standing up to each challenge with reliable people by your side.

Success for Everyone

One of the fears that some people have when it comes to working together with others is the thought that they will lose out on some of the reward if they share responsibilities along the way. In reality, there is more than enough success to go around – but you have to get there first. Chances are, you are never going to reach the point where you feel successful if you are unwilling to take on teammates along the way. Everyone in your group can be successful, but only if you band together and stick it out through the tough times ahead.

Never Betray a Teammate

SEALs are loyal to the very end. Even if there is a disagreement within the team, you won't see a SEAL turn his back on a fellow team member. In fact, it is quite the opposite. A SEAL will go to the ends of the earth in order to support and protect his teammate, and you should have the same attitude towards those who are working with you. If you are going to be trusted, you have to be trustworthy – that might sound like an obvious point, but it is important. A SEAL is going to be loyal to his teammate because he knows with 100% confidence that his teammates will be loyal to his as well. If you don't give off that impression to those around you, it will be impossible to get the kind of loyalty that you desire. Prove that you will stand by your associates no matter what and they will be far more likely to give you their best.

The Mastermind Group

The concept of a mastermind group is to bring together a group of people who all have knowledge and expertise in specific areas. When you have such a group assembled, each member can contribute something unique and the whole will be greater than the sum of the parts. For instance, imagine that you are starting a business in a field where you would consider yourself an expert. While you can rely on your own knowledge within the specific field, there are many other parts of business that you may not know – such as marketing, accounting, management, etc. By assembling a mastermind team to help you develop the business, each member with their own strengths, you can compile a whole business plan that is far stronger than anything you could have assembled on your own.

Learn More to Earn More

You should never be done learning in life. It doesn't matter what the topic might be, or what kind of experience and education you have, the process of learning is never finished. You can always get better, and you can always add to what you know. While the SEALs are considered the premier force in the world for completing vital military missions, they are not perfect and they do not know it all. In fact, if there were to assume they knew everything, they would be opening themselves up to unnecessary risk. By staying humble and maintaining a desire to learn, they can remain on top of their game for years to come.

In your case, being willing to learn means you will open up more and more possibilities to make more money. It is easy to put a cap on your potential by holding firm in your knowledge and closing off to new ideas. Innovation should be welcomed in your mind, and you should seek out new ways to look at the same old problems. If you are unwilling to learn and adapt, somebody else will – and they will quickly be enjoying the success you could have had.

Chapter Seven – Success Starts with Self-Discipline

The pain is coming. Whether you like it or not, whether you are ready to deal with it or not, you are going to have to feel some pain on the way to success. For SEALs, that pain starts with the BUD/s training process that they go through right up front. For you, it might be the long hours that you have to put in to get your business off the ground, or the frugal lifestyle that you have to lead in order to save up enough money to launch your company. Whatever it is, success never comes without sacrifice – it's just that simple.

So, when do you want to feel that pain? For the SEALs, the answer is easy – they suffer upfront in the way of brutal training sessions and long hours so that they are prepared for the battle in the field. If they don't feel the pain now, they will feel in later in the form of regret when they realize they are underprepared for the task at hand. Of course, that would never happen to a SEAL, but it could happen to you.

Pressure Reveals Preparation

"When you're under pressure, you don't rise to the occasion, you sink to the level of your training".

That is a perfect way to sum up why you should work so hard to be prepared for anything you may encounter. You shouldn't count on being able to get the job done when the time comes to rise to the challenge. Instead, you should put in enough preparation that you are sure you will be able to meet any demand that may be asked of you in the real world. Surprises always come up in real life, and it is your level of discipline and preparation that will determine how you handle those challenges. A disciplined individual will be able to meet the challenges head-on, while someone who lacks preparation will likely go running in the other direction.

The last thing you want to do is position yourself for success, only to find that you haven't done the work necessary to actually reach out and grab it. Think about it this way – a Navy SEAL would not want to arrive in the field in a perfect position to defeat the enemy, only to find that he isn't physically fit enough to complete the mission. The preparation in terms of conditioning needs to have been done long ago so that there is nothing holding him back when the time comes to perform. While your path to success might not require a certain level of physical fitness, it is certainly going to demand preparation in some form. Ready yourself as early as possible and you will be able to rise to the occasion.

No Detail Too Small

When you are going through your preparation process – no matter what you are preparing for – there is no detail that is too small to consider. The SEALs are famous for their attention to even the smallest of details, which is exactly why they have such an impressive resume. Instead of taking the minor parts of a mission for granted, SEALs pore over every last detail until they are sure they are ready for everything that could come their way.

This is a mantra that you can easily take into your own life. It is easy to take some of the smaller parts of your process for granted, especially if they are things that you have done before. Don't fall into that trap. As the saying goes, 'the devil is in the details'. You can easily be tripped up by seemingly small details that become major problems down the line. Pay close attention to all of the various parts of your process, and you will be that much closer to success thanks to your efforts.

Never Get Comfortable

Many people work hard looking forward to the day that they can get comfortable and just cruise. If that sounds like your line of thinking, you might find this next point to be a bit disappointing – that day isn't coming. There will never be a day in which you can afford to get complacent or satisfied with your progress, unless you want to get passed by the competition. No matter what field you are in, there is always someone who is nipping at your heels. For the SEALs, that competition comes in the form of younger SEALs who are hungry for the chance to prove themselves. If a veteran SEAL goes into 'coast mode' and just decides to take it easy for a while, they are sure to be passed up by someone who is working harder and is more dedicated to the cause. For you to be successful in your own pursuits, you too have to be completely dedicated to the task at hand.

Speaking of being uncomfortable, there is a good reason that the SEALs are so good at thriving when conditions are difficult – because they have been there before. Take the example of the 'sugar cookie'. This is a particularly brutal training technique designed to keep students as uncomfortable as possible, all day long. According to Admiral William McRaven –

"The student had to run, fully clothed, into the surf zone and then, wet from head to toe, roll around on the beach until every part of their body was covered with sand. They stayed in that uniform the rest of the day – cold, wet, and sandy".

Simply put, that sounds brutal. Everyone knows the feeling of having sand stuck to their body after a day at the beach, and it is not a good feeling to be sure. The level of discomfort when completing this type of training is hard to imagine for someone who has never been through it. Of course, the reason they do this kind of training is to prepare SEALs for what might lie ahead out in the field. If they wind up in a brutal situation with no relief in sight, the SEALs will know they can handle it because they have been there before.

Chapter Eight – Never Ring the Bell

The process of becoming a Navy SEAL might seem extremely complicated, but it can actually be boiled down to one very simple point – don't ring the bell. If you don't ring the bell, you will become a Navy SEAL. Of course, that is incredibly hard to do, and the majority of people who enter SEAL training wind up ringing that bell at some point.

So what is the bell? The bell is the indication of giving up – it is how you quit. If you just can't take it anymore, you simply ring the bell and it is all over. You are dismissed from training, and you no longer have to go through the hell that is the SEAL training process. With that said, ringing the bell means that you are not going to reach the goal of becoming a Navy SEAL. Giving up means relief from the pain, but it also means falling short of success.

You are likely not going to encounter any brutal physical training in your life like that which the SEALs are subjected to during BUD/s. However, you can still learn a great lesson from the concept of ringing the bell. Are you going to ring the bell in your day to day life? Are you going to give up on yourself short of the goals that you have laid out? Are you going to take shortcuts while trying to build your career instead of doing everything the right (and difficult) way?

One of the challenges that you face is that you will only be accountable to yourself in most situations. Prospective SEALs have superiors to keep them to their schedule, and to demand the best of them from start to finish. Most likely, you will not have that kind of leadership in front of you. Rather, you will need to motivate yourself to provide the best of what you have to offer each day. As Admiral McRaven said, "If you want to change the world, don't ever, ever ring the bell."

The less of this section is beautiful in Its simplicity – just don't ring the bell. If you don't ring the bell, success should be soon to follow.

Comfort Zone

Most of us are stuck in a routine. Routines can become a rut. We can easily get stuck in these ruts and forget how we ever got there to begin with. We are also on our own journey. For some of us this journey is really difficult but that is just how it needs to be at first. Most people refuse their journey and choose an easier path. You must accept your journey. You need to challenge yourself to leave your comfort zone and take on your journey.

You cannot improve if you're on autopilot. You need to set goals that are well beyond the outer limits of your comfort zone. You need to get out of the complacency of the routine.

The comfort zone becomes your norm. It stops you from gaining experience, knowledge and gaining mental toughness.

"You're not here to survive this, you're here to take charge of it."

There are too many people that are simply trying to survive in life – in fact, you may be one of those people as you read this book. The goal, rather than just trying to get by, should be trying to take charge and thrive in your life. What do you want out of life? What do you want to accomplish? Whatever it is that is on your list, the right mindset and the right attitude is going to be crucial to your success. By taking a page from the most dangerous men on the planet, you can take a huge step in the right direction.

Chapter Nine – Elite Warrior Success Principles

There are very few truly elite warriors. There are plenty of people who would like to live up to this standard, but few are able to actually rise to the occasion when it matters most. Being an elite warrior requires tremendous physical strength, calm thinking under pressure, tremendous preparation, and an overall commitment to the mission. It might be easy enough to find people with one or two of the traits needed to be an elite warrior, but finding the whole package is rare indeed.

This section is going to highlight three of the main principles that are adhered to by the truly elite warriors.

Take on the Sharks

When the SEALs are engaging in the swimming portion of their training, they do so off the coast of San Clemente, California. In addition to being a beautiful location, this spot is also notable for being a breeding ground for sharks. Rather than being told to turn and swim quickly in the other direction when encountering a shark, SEALs are told to deal with them face on. They are not to act afraid, and they are to strike the shark directly in the snout if attacked.

Think about that. When faced with one of the fiercest predators in the world, a Navy SEAL in training is told to meet the challenge by punching the shark in the face. That is the definition of not running away from your problems. After all, there is no way to outswim a shark in his own territory, so confronting the challenge with a punch in the face is the best a SEAL can do to survive.

Hopefully, you won't have to face any actual sharks in your future. However, you are certain to face people who try to bully you around in order to get their way. When you face a bully, don't turn and run – stand up for yourself and take them head on. That doesn't mean supplying them with a punch in the face, of course, but you still need to make sure you aren't backing down as a habit. Successful people don't tuck their tails and run when the going gets tough – they rise to the occasion and make sure they hold their ground.

Give More to Get More

Even a top warrior, who is as self-reliant as anyone in the world, will still lean on others for help and support. The best way to do this is to give more of yourself to others, because you will get more in return. Instead of only trying to get as much as you can from others, do your best to give of yourself in every situation possible. This is the SEAL way, as they work hard to make sure their teammates are taken care of at every turn.

It isn't always a natural choice to give to others when you are trying to push yourself to success. This is when you need to take a step back and take a look at the big picture. Yes, you want to be successful, but you want to be successful in a way that is going to last for the long run. Pushing people out of your way in a dash to the top isn't going to build a foundation for long-term success. Instead, your strategy should be based on constantly giving of yourself with the good of everyone around you in mind. Doing so will build relationships and partnerships that will last, and everyone should be able to succeed as the years go by.

Identify the Moment that Matters

Training to become a SEAL is scary stuff – but perhaps nothing is quite as scary as learning how to approach an enemy ship. This is a training maneuver that is completed at night, alone, underneath a steel ship that blocks out all of the ambient light. Starting with a two-mile underwater swim, the SEAL must then find just the right spot under the boat. Turning again to Admiral McRaven for an explanation –

"The steel structure of the ship blocks out the moonlight – it blocks the surrounding street lamps – it blocks all ambient light. To be successful in your mission, you have to swim under the ship and find the keep – the center line and the deepest part of the ship."

While consistency is a great thing, there are certain moments in life that demand you rise to the occasion. For a SEAL, this dark training mission is one such moment. Will you rise to the occasion when you face your own dark challenge on your way to success, or will you abort the mission and seek out the light as quickly as possible? The willingness to fight through the dark in order to achieve your mission is what will determine your ultimate success or failure.

Conclusion

Success comes easy for no one. That holds true for the Navy SEALs, for the richest people in the world, and for everyone else. If you want to be successful, you are going to have to work for it. Without the commitment to work and to stick with your process even when the going is tough, you will never reach your goals – it really is that simple.

If you would like to dedicate yourself to success and you are willing to put in the work, you can learn a lot by following the lead of the Navy SEALs. The SEALs are the very definition of success, as each member has earned his spot through incredibly difficult training from both a mental and physical standpoint. While the physical challenges that the SEALs have to deal with will not be something that you face in your life (hopefully), the way they persevere in the face of a challenge can certainly teach you a lot about life in general.

In this book, we have walked through some of the basic fundamentals of the SEALs, in terms of how they think and what they must do to be successful. From this point, it is going to be up to you to apply these lessons to your own life. Everyone has their own unique goals, and their own unique challenges that they will face on the way to reaching those goals. Only you know what kind of road you face ahead – so only you can decide how to apply the lessons that the SEALs teach to your own life.

It is my hope that you have gained perspective from this book, and that this new perspective will help you as you are trying to move closer and closer to success. I truly believe that everyone has success hidden within them somewhere, and it only takes hard work and dedication to a vision to bring it to the surface. Thank you for taking the time to read, and I wish you nothing but the best in your pursuit of the goals that will define your life!

The SEAL Code

- Loyalty to Country, Team and Teammate
- Serve with Honor and Integrity On and Off the Battlefield
- Ready to Lead, Ready to Follow, Never Quit
- Take responsibility for your actions and the actions of your teammates
- Excel as Warriors through Discipline and Innovation
- Train for War, Fight to Win, Defeat our Nation's Enemies
- Earn your Trident everyday

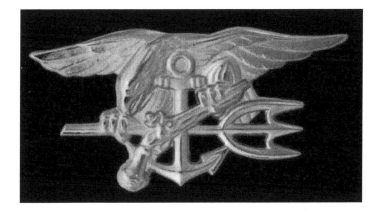

Made in the USA
Lexington, KY
14 February 2017